Nihil Obstat: Fr. Philip-Michael F. Tangorra, S.T.L.
Censor Librorum
Imprimatur: + Most Rev. Arthur J. Serratelli, S.T.D., S.S.L., D.D.
Bishop of Paterson
December 26, 2015

Text © 2016 by THE REGINA PRESS
an imprint of Catholic Book Publishing Corp.
77 West End Road
Totowa, NJ 07512

Illustrations: Marifé González
Illustrations © SUSAETA EDICIONES, S.A.
(RG14650)
ISBN: 978-0-88271-394-6   CPSIA February 2016   10 9 8 7 6 5 4 3 2 1 S/S

Printed in India
www.catholicbookpublishing.com

Children's Bedtime Prayers

Regina Press

It's Bedtime

AS I get into bed,
I thank you, my Angel,
for watching over me.
With you near me,
I feel very safe.
How blessed am I
to have my very own
Guardian Angel.

BEFORE I sleep, Guardian Angel,
help me to thank God.
Thank You, God the Father, for the
wonderful world You made.
Thank You, God the Son, for dying
and rising to save me from my sins.
Thank You, God the Holy Spirit,
Who was sent to make me holy.

THANK you, Guardian Angel,
for reminding me of my Faith
all during the day today.
You remind me to give good
example to my friends.
You remind me to think of God
no matter where I am—
at home, at school, at play.

God Sent My Guardian Angel to Me

DEAR Guardian Angel,
I know that God sent you
just to be with me.

He trusted you
to stay by my side,
to protect me from harm,
to help me learn about the Faith.

I feel you with me every day,
and I know God couldn't
have sent me a better Angel friend.

YOU, my Guardian Angel,
are my constant companion.
I know you will be with me
as soon as I wake up.
You will be with me,
whether I choose to do
right or wrong.
You will be with me as
I pray and as I play.
God knew you would never
leave my side and would help
to bring me closer to Him.

Prayer of Protection

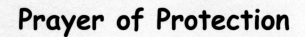

DEAR Mary, Mother of God,
I pray to you this night
to watch over me as I sleep.
As you protected the
Baby Jesus as He slept,
please keep me safe.

I pray, too, that you will
watch over my parents,
my brothers and sisters,
and all those I love.

The Our Father

OUR Father, Who art in heaven,
hallowed be Thy name;
Thy Kingdom come,
Thy will be done
on earth as it is in heaven.
Give us this day our daily bread,
and forgive us our trespasses,
as we forgive those who trespass
     against us;
and lead us not into temptation,
but deliver us from evil.
Amen.

The Hail Mary

MY Guardian Angel, you help me to love Mary as my Mother. I pray to her with these words:

Hail, Mary, full of grace!
The Lord is with you;
blessed are you among women,
and blessed is the fruit
of your womb, Jesus.

Holy Mary, Mother of God,
pray for us sinners,
now and at the hour of our death. Amen.

19

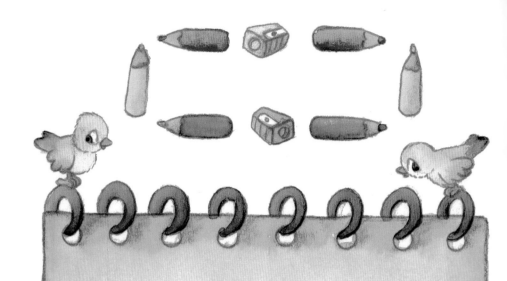

DEAR Guardian Angel,
thank you for being with me
while I was at school today.

I know you are never
far from me
no matter what I am doing.

You helped me
to listen to my teacher and
to behave as I should.

I like having you with me there!

Just Playing

SWEET Guardian Angel,
thank you for protecting me
while I was at play today.

I felt you near me
as my friends and I
were having fun.

I think you being there
made playing even more fun!

Guardian Angel, You Were Watching

1, 2, 3...
You looked at me.

4, 5, 6, 7...
She's running to win.

8, 9, 10...
She made a new friend.

25

Giving Thanks

HEAVENLY Father, thank You
for the life You gave me
and for all Your many gifts.

Thank You for my Faith,
the Sacraments, and the
Commandments.

Thank You for my family,
and for the love we share.

Thank You for all You have created
to make the world beautiful.

Night Prayer to My Guardian Angel

ANGEL of God,
my Guardian dear,
God's love for me
has sent you here.

Ever this night
be at my side,
to love and guard,
to watch over and abide.

My dear Guardian Angel,
keep me from all danger
and lead me to heaven.
Amen.

Help Me with My Fears, Guardian Angel

I'M afraid I'm
not showing God
how much I love Him.
I'm afraid I'm
not pleasing my parents.
I'm afraid I'm
not doing well enough
in school.

I pray for your help with my fears.
I so want to love God, obey my parents,
and do well in my studies.

I'm Sorry

MY Guardian Angel,
I'm really sorry for . . .
* not cleaning my room
  like Mom asked.
* making my little sister
  cry when I scared her.
* making my teacher mad
  by talking in class.
Please help me to do
better tomorrow.

Thank You, Guardian Angel

THANK you, my Angel,
for helping me enjoy all of
God's good gifts—
Jesus as my Friend,
my parents who love me,
the friends that I play with.

Not to mention the birds' song,
the flowers I smell,
the warmth of the sun,
blue skies and puffy clouds—
and even raindrops.

Blessings

SPIRIT of God, please bless:

* my whole family

* my friends

* our Church

* my teachers

* our country

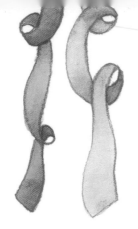

Thank You, God, for Today

DEAR God, I thank You for today and for each day of my life.

Today has been a gift from You.
I hope I have used it well to
serve both You and others.

Thank You for each birthday that makes me think of Your love for me.

Someday, I hope to join You in heaven.

Words That Make Me Think of God When I Pray

Love

Mercy

Forgiveness

Goodness

Hope

Faith
Soul

Kindness

Joy
Thanks
Praise

Blessing
Grace
Peace
Truth

41

Remembering Others

BESIDES those who are close to me,
I want to pray for
those I don't know—
the homeless, the hungry,
the lonely, the hopeless, the poor,
the soldiers who protect us.
Please, God, keep them in
Your care.

Jesus said in Matthew 19:14. . .

"LET the little children come to me, and do not stop them. For it is to such as these that the kingdom of heaven belongs."

I pray, Jesus, that heaven will be my eternal reward. Amen.